Original title:
Big Bang Ballads

Copyright © 2025 Creative Arts Management OÜ
All rights reserved.

Author: Theodore Sinclair
ISBN HARDBACK: 978-1-80567-771-0
ISBN PAPERBACK: 978-1-80567-892-2

Cosmic Refrain

In the beginning, a playful spark,
Atoms danced, igniting the dark.
Stars giggled, and planets rolled,
The universe hummed, a tale retold.

Galaxies swirled in a comical chase,
Nebulas puffed like they were in a race.
Gravity's tug, a silly waltz,
As comets plotted their next crazy vaults.

Vibration of Worlds

Waves of laughter across the void,
Cosmic jokes that can't be destroyed.
Asteroids wearing top hats, so grand,
Jovial moons that wobbled and planned.

Every quasar bursts into song,
Strumming chords that last too long.
Each tick of time, a punchline clear,
Cosmic puns that never disappear.

Geometries of Sound

Shapes that echo in a rhythmic spree,
Cylinders bounce, triangles agree.
Sines and cosines in playful fights,
Singing their songs on starry nights.

Curves that twist and angles that bend,
Mathematical gags that never end.
The galaxy giggles at every note,
In this wacky symphony, we all float.

Echoing Through Eternity

In the depths where silence dwells,
Echoes gather as laughter swells.
Ripples of joy in spacetime's weave,
Tickling the void, we can't believe.

The cosmos chuckles, a cosmic jest,
Eternal punchlines, never at rest.
With each echo, a wink from afar,
In the universe's heart, we find who we are.

Harmonies from the Galactic Forge

In the depths where stars are born,
Gas clouds dance, quite forlorn.
An asteroid tumbles, quite a sight,
Just dodged a comet, yikes! What a fright!

Planets spin on a cosmic whim,
With rings that gleam, oh so grim.
A moon trips over its own feet,
In this space ballet, we can't be beat!

Cosmic Chords of Creation

Singing stars with their dazzling glow,
Harmonizing in an endless show.
The universe laughs, it's having such fun,
While black holes dance, oh what a run!

Galaxies twirl, in playful delight,
With dark matter hiding from the light.
The cosmos giggles with each supernova,
As aliens join in, a wild takeover!

Lightyears of Lament

Floating through time, oh what a chore,
Dodging meteors, I swore!
A lightyear feels like an endless chat,
Where's the coffee? And where's the cat?

Stars whisper secrets, but none make sense,
While gravity plays its funny suspense.
Comets crash, causing a scene,
I'm stuck in space, feeling quite mean!

The Symphony of Everything

Strings of spacetime pluck and twang,
As the universe hums its cosmic clang.
Nebulas swirl in a jazzy beat,
While quasars jump up to tap their feet.

Wormholes wink, a cheeky jest,
As time skips like a dance contest.
With planets jiving, quite the spree,
Our universe throws the best dance party!

Radiance of Infinity

In a flash, all was bright,
Stars danced with pure delight.
Galaxies took their first spin,
Laughing at where they'd been.

Time took a giant leap,
Creation began to creep.
Planets formed with a jig,
Who knew space could be so big?

Eons passed with a cheer,
Matter waltzed, no fear.
Black holes wore a funny wig,
Drawing in all, oh so big!

Laughter echoed through the night,
As cosmos built its playful sight.
From chaos, order did rise,
A universe full of surprise.

The First Light's Lullaby

Whispers in the cosmic breeze,
Light began with utmost ease.
Singing softly, stars would hum,
To the universe, oh what fun!

The fabric stretched, oh so wide,
With giggles from the cosmic tide.
Nebulas in colors bright,
Rocked the cradle of the night.

Gravity pulled with a tease,
Creating orbits as it pleased.
Planets twirled, oh what a show,
In this dance, they took a bow.

As comets raced with tails aflame,
Every fragment played a game.
In the dark, a song was spun,
Starlight shone, and all was fun.

Cosmic Serenade

From a tiny speck of dust,
Came a symphony of rust.
Sound waves echoed, bright and clear,
Galactic tunes for all to hear.

Strings of stars and twinkling sprites,
Played a tune on cosmic nights.
Harmony in vacuum vast,
A melody that spells the past.

Timekeepers of the grand design,
Counted laughs, oh how they shine.
In every orbit, every sway,
Music of the cosmos play.

Planets in a crazy race,
Joined the rhythm, set the pace.
In this orchestra divine,
Creation danced with pure sunshine.

Nebula's Song

In a cloud of colors bright,
Nebula sang with all her might.
With a wink from a distant star,
She reminded us just how far.

Her gas and dust began to swirl,
Creating laughter, watch it whirl.
A nursery for stars anew,
Giggling as they burst on through.

In each corner of the night,
Whispers shimmered, pure delight.
From chaos came a vibrant show,
As cosmic winds began to blow.

With a chuckle, she took her bow,
As supernovas shouted WOW!
In the vastness, joy took flight,
Nebula's song a pure delight.

The Unraveling of Time

In the beginning, it all went pop,
Stars spinning out, no time to stop.
A cosmic sneeze, oh what a sight,
Galaxies laughing in pure delight.

Black holes dance with a wobble and twist,
Time went nuts, but who could resist?
A quirk of fate, a twist of fate,
Einstein chuckles, 'Ain't it great?'

Celestial Sparks

Shooting stars wish for extra cheese,
While comets laugh in a cosmic breeze.
Planets wobble, trying to break,
Their long-standing dance, for goodness' sake!

Asteroids roam, playing tag in space,
With a wink and a twist, they quicken their pace.
Jupiter snores, while Saturn spins rings,
In a universe filled with wondrous things.

Cosmic Dreams

Nebulae swirl like cotton candy clouds,
Dreamers in space get lost in the crowds.
Galactic giggles echo in the night,
As meteors bounce, oh what a flight!

Aliens dance in their glow-in-the-dark suits,
With funky tunes from their cosmic roots.
They boogie 'round stars, in ultimate glee,
Inviting us all to join in the spree!

Journey Through the Void

Rockets zooming, like bees in a hive,
Through the dark void, they wiggle and jive.
Cosmic travelers with snacks in tow,
On a quest for laughter, through space they go!

Wormholes grin with a cheeky surprise,
As travelers spin, with wide-open eyes.
Across the vastness, they twirl and sway,
In the funny dance of the Milky Way!

The Velocity of Light

In the cosmos, with a wink,
Stars go zooming in a blink.
Light-years crossed in a race,
Oh, what a hilarious space!

Aliens laugh at our slow pace,
With their speed, they win the chase.
Photon cars zoom and glide,
With joy, they take a ride!

Galactic Echo

Hear the planets giggle and cheer,
As comets fly past with a sneer.
Asteroids dance in a line,
Bumping into space, oh, so fine!

Echoes of laughter rings so bright,
In the shadow of the moonlight.
Gravity pulls, but they won't fall,
Singing together, they have a ball!

Celestial Rhythms

Dancing moons in a cosmic groove,
Swinging stars, they know how to move.
In the vacuum, the bass is strong,
A celestial DJ plays all night long!

Planets twirl, in a merry spin,
Laughter erupts, a galactic din.
Rhythms echo, a cosmic tune,
Even black holes laugh under the moon!

Harmony of the Heavens

In the sky, a choir sings loud,
Celestial beings form a crowd.
With harmonies that tickle the air,
Even meteors stop to share!

Shooting stars make wishes in jest,
While galaxies play, they never rest.
A symphony of laughs through space,
In the end, we're all in this race!

Harmony in Chaos

In a swirl of dust, a laugh erupts,
Stars collide, and no one interrupts.
Planets wobble in their silly prance,
Gravity's playing the jokester's dance.

Galaxies twirl like marionette strings,
Comets zoom past, wearing bright bling.
A universe filled with giggling sparks,
As quasars play tag in the cosmic parks.

Celestial Dance

Neutron stars waltz on a cosmic floor,
Pulsars blink out like a dance hall's roar.
Black holes spin with a chuckle so deep,
While space dust shimmies and sweeps to the beat.

Planets cartwheel through the Milky Way,
Emojis in orbit, on cosmic display.
Saturn's rings laugh in a glittery hue,
In this universe, there's nothing to rue.

Cosmic Rhapsody

A symphony plays from the void's embrace,
With giggles of gas and the light's quick race.
Echoes of laughter float through the night,
Harmonies twinkling, a joyous delight.

Shooting stars serenade the dark sky,
Tickling the heavens as they zip by.
While asteroids bounce like they're in a game,
In this cosmic concert, nothing's the same.

Birth Rhythms

From the chaos, a chuckle ignites,
Stars are born with the funniest sights.
Nebulae wink in their misty attire,
Sprinkling giggles like celestial fire.

With every burst, a new rhythm starts,
Gravity giggles and steals our hearts.
In the cradle of cosmos, what a delight,
New worlds spin in the soft cosmic light.

Universe in Tune

In the void where atoms dance,
Stars twirl in a cosmic prance.
Galaxies giggle, comets chase,
Gravity's pulling on their face.

Nebulae puff like cotton candy,
While quasars beam, all bright and dandy.
Whirling planets, they sing aloud,
Making the universe feel so proud.

Celestial Unity

In a starry jam, the suns all hum,
Moonbeams shine, inviting the fun.
And if you listen, oh so clear,
You'll hear black holes laugh, oh dear!

The Milky Way's a dance floor grand,
With asteroids in a conga band.
Supernovas pop, confetti flies,
In this cosmic party, laughter ties.

Ballads of the Cosmos

Planets pluck their strings with grace,
Singing songs of a timeless space.
Wormholes wink and say, 'Hey there!'
As pulsars thrum without a care.

Stardust falls like glittering rain,
Spreading joy throughout our domain.
When the universe strikes a chord,
Even the comets can't be ignored.

The Harmonic Burst

A burst of laughter from the stars,
Echoes linger, fun from afar.
Quarks and leptons play a game,
Creating laws that feel the same.

From dark matter's sneak, oh what a tease,
To the light-years traveled with cosmic ease.
In every twinkle, a joke resides,
As the universe spins with laughter, it glides.

Songs of the Cosmos

In the sky, where planets play,
Comets dance, hip-hip-hooray!
Galaxies twirl with much delight,
They do the moonwalk every night.

Asteroids shout, 'We're not so small!'
While black holes sip from cosmic wall.
The universe sings a silly tune,
As aliens hum to the light of the moon.

Stars are winking, oh what a sight,
They gossip late into the night.
With every twinkle, a joke is cracked,
In space's party, no fun is lacked!

From dust to planets, the fun does grow,
As supernovas put on quite the show.
Let's join the cosmic, raucous cheer,
And dance our way to the end of the year!

Astral Overture

A cosmic choir, voices loud,
Remember, they're just a cloud!
Shooting stars, take aim and fire,
With wishes that never tire.

Planets spin in their fancy shoes,
While sunbeams play peek-a-boo blues.
A cosmic laugh, a galaxy joke,
As nebulas swirl in colorful cloak.

Light-years pass as comets glide,
They race each other, full of pride.
Black holes chuckle, 'Where'd they go?'
As galaxies whirl, they steal the show!

Yet in this vast, fun universe,
Every twinkle's a poetic verse.
Join the laughter, don't be shy,
For cosmic joy will never die!

Whirlwind of Stars

In a whirlwind, stars collide,
Spinning tales, they're full of pride.
Galaxies giggle as they twist,
In the cosmic dance, you can't resist.

A neutron star's a heavy weight,
Cracking jokes at an asteroid's fate.
With cosmic puns, they light the dark,
While nova blooms like a fireworks spark.

Comets slide with a swish and a grin,
Saying, 'Catch me if you can, come on in!'
Stars conspire, a playful plot,
To paint the cosmos with laughter's dot.

So raise your glass, toast the night,
For every twinkle's pure delight.
The universe is a comedy stage,
Where every dance brings a new age!

The Melodic Void

In the void, there's a tune so sweet,
As cosmic critters tap their feet.
Asteroids jive, comets slide,
In a dance that won't abide.

Galactic giggles echo so clear,
As quasars clap, a cosmic cheer.
Dancing stardust fills the air,
With every twist, a wacky dare.

The universe hums an upbeat song,
While planets whirl and spin along.
Supernovae paint the sky bright,
In a colorful rave, oh, what a sight!

So grab your partner, cosmic ball,
There's laughter and joy for one and all.
In the melodic void we reside,
Where fun and mischief collide.

The Infinite Composition

Once there was a cosmic sneeze,
Atoms danced with style and ease.
A burst of light, a glittered grin,
The universe began to spin.

Planets twirled like playful cats,
Galaxies in funny hats.
Distant stars flickered, said, "Hello!"
As dark matter joined the show.

In laughter of celestial glee,
Comets darted — whee! Whee! Whee!
Black holes burped, a cosmic joke,
In vastness vast, the cosmos spoke.

Songs of the Celestial Seas

Waves of stardust crash and play,
Moonbeams dance in a bright ballet.
Jupiter spins with a twinkling toe,
Neptune sings, where did time go?

Stars bubble like cosmic soup,
Celestial creatures form a loop.
Asteroids rock out like they're mad,
While supernovae shout, "Ain't that bad!"

Galaxies splash in colors so bright,
In the cosmic ocean, pure delight.
A whale of a tale in the void of space,
While planets giggle, keeping pace.

Chasing Starlight

Chasing starlight, what a race,
Falling comets break the space.
Light years pass with a wink and blink,
As cosmic runners share a wink.

Aliens play a game of tag,
With Saturn's rings, they love to brag.
Who knew that moons could also dance,
In the vastness of that cosmic chance?

Shooting stars screaming, "Catch me fast!"
Laughter echoes from the past.
In a universe with endless skill,
Chasing starlight gives a thrill.

Awash in Nebula

In a cloud of colors, swirling bright,
Stardust giggles through the night.
A nebula winks, says, "Join the fun!"
Make a wish on a shooting one.

Fairy tales spun in cobwebs of stars,
Cosmic critters chase their cars.
Riding comets down the lane,
Spinning circles, avoiding rain.

Through the cosmos, artists roam,
Painting galaxies to call home.
A laugh here, a light there shines,
Awash in nebula, joy entwines.

The Dawn of Everything

In the beginning, nothing was clear,
Just a cosmic joke, full of cheer.
Tiny particles danced, what a sight,
As atoms wobbled in pure delight.

Galaxies spun like tops on a string,
Planets giggled, oh, what a fling!
Stars burst forth, in a wild display,
Creating chaos in a cosmic ballet.

Dark matter hid behind bright things,
Playing tricks like mischievous kings.
A universe tossed with glee and surprise,
Winking softly with twinkling eyes.

From nothing to all, what a grand plot,
Twirling around in a cosmic thought.
The dawn of everything birthed a name,
In this universe, we play a game.

Starlit Serenades

Under a blanket of shimmering stars,
Aliens hum along to their guitars.
They serenade comets in swift, bright arcs,
While asteroids groove, sharing their sparks.

Laser beams dance in the cosmic air,
Soundtrack of giggles—oh, what a pair!
Planets twist in rhythm, a jovial sight,
As moons spin around in sheer delight.

Meteors slide down like soap on the floor,
With popcorn clouds just waiting for more.
Astrophysics? Nah, it's just a big show,
A celestial carnival where laughter can grow.

So join in the fun, don't be shy,
Gaze at the cosmos and let your heart fly.
The universe croons with joy and play,
In starlit serenades, come laugh away!

Echoes in the Void

In the silence, echoes bounce around,
Making friends with the lost and found.
Black holes chuckle as they swallow light,
While galaxies whisper secrets at night.

Quasars shout in colorful bursts,
While comets zoom past, quenching their thirst.
The void plays tag, no need for a score,
Hiding behind stars, craving some more.

Cosmic echoes giggle, floating so free,
Warning asteroids, "Watch out for me!"
Each twinkle of light tells a pun or two,
In the expanding dark, fun never feels through.

So listen closely, hear the cosmic tease,
The void's just a playground, with laughter to seize.
In these echoes of space, rejoice and unwind,
For every moment, a new truth we'll find.

Cosmic Cradle

In the cradle of space, where dreams take flight,
The universe rocks like a child in the night.
Galactic lullabies sung soft and low,
With stars as the lights in a grand light show.

Nebulas swirl like candy floss skies,
While planets make wishes with twinkling eyes.
Floating on asteroids, we laugh and play,
In this cosmic cradle, we dance all day.

Meteor showers sprinkle giggles and glee,
As stardust whispers, "Just come with me!"
The sun waves goodbye with a cheeky grin,
While moons have a party, let the fun begin!

Cosmic swaddles wrap us in love,
As comets wink down from the heavens above.
In this cradle, we find our place,
In the universe's heart, we embrace the space.

Illuminating the Abyss

A light bulb flicks on, in a cosmic dance,
Galaxies stumble, like they're in a trance.
Stars playing tag in a darkening sky,
Laughing and whirling, oh my, oh my!

Planets all wobbly, like toys on a string,
Rockets with hiccups start to take wing.
Gravity's giggle, pulling us down,
They're spinning in circles, oh what a clown!

A comet trips over a cosmic bed,
With glittering dust, it's a sparkling spread.
Neptune's got jokes, he's a real funny guy,
While Saturn just chuckles and gives us a sigh.

In this vast bazaar of the universe wide,
Laughter erupts as the stars take a ride.
With a wink and a nod, they twirl and they sway,
In a show so delightful, come join the play!

Tides of Time

Time's a surfer on a cosmic wave,
Riding the currents, so bold, so brave.
Past and future mixed in a wild fashion,
Tick-tock's a joke, no need for compassion.

Yesterday's pudding is jiggling still,
While tomorrow's laughter gives it a thrill.
Moments are prancing in a slapstick spree,
Taking a dive in the cosmic sea.

The clocks all wobble, they seem to have fun,
Playing leapfrog beneath the bright sun.
Every second's a punchline just waiting to land,
With giggles that echo across the vast strand.

In this merry whirl of the tick and the tock,
Time's just a jester, a paradox clock.
While we dance through the waves, just take it in stride,
Join the laughter and let joy be your guide!

Chords of Creation

Banjos and violins in a cosmic jam,
Strings humming sounds like a big cosmic spam.
Galaxies strumming on the chords of the night,
Melodies twirl, oh what a delight!

A symphony stumbles, overtures hop,
As planets play maracas, they can't make it stop.
Rhythms collide in a funky parade,
Dancing through stardust, a musical charade.

A saxophone sings as it floats through the dark,
While meteors bop with a marvelous spark.
Harmony bounces in a mad, crazy way,
Creating a racket where music can play.

In this orchestra grand, we laugh and we cheer,
As chaos plays on, with joy crystal clear.
With each note ringing out from this cosmic hall,
Join the laughter, the song of it all!

Sounds of the Infinite

Echoes are giggling, the void takes a breath,
Whispers of stardust are teasing with death.
Voices of comets, they make quite a fuss,
In this boundless place, oh come ride the bus!

Bubbles of laughter pop in a line,
While asteroids honk like they're waiting for time.
Singing in silence, the cosmos does hum,
With a wink from a quasar, the fun's just begun!

Vibrations of joy bouncing off every wall,
Planets are lengthening their cosmic crawl.
Riding the echoes, we giggle and spin,
In a playground of sounds, let the madness begin!

Through echoes of chaos, we float and we fly,
In the grandest of jesters, the stars wink the eye.
Join in the laughter, don't let it go thin,
In this infinite realm, the joy's always in!

Cosmic Rhapsody in Motion

In the beginning, chaos reigned bright,
Atoms were dancing, a wild starry sight.
Gases were giggling, swirling around,
What a comedy show, in the void without sound!

A neutron tripped, a proton laughed loud,
The universe cracked up, drawing a crowd.
Floating in space, a joke or two,
Even black holes chuckled at the view!

Planets were born, made of dust and dreams,
Stars shot confetti, bursting at the seams.
Gravity waltzed, pulled them along,
Syncing to rhythms of a cosmic song!

And so they danced, in this grandeur so fun,
Life's cosmic giggle had only begun.
Join in the laughter, let worries all cease,
In this jolly ballet of vastness and peace!

Whispers of Primal Energy

Whispers of atoms, too playful to keep,
Huddling together, secrets run deep.
A quark told a joke, the others would cheer,
Giggles erupted, the universe near!

From darkness emerged, a flamboyant flare,
Electric socks on, with wild cosmic hair.
Let's spin a tale of particles bright,
Shooting star laughter that tickles the night!

Sing songs of fusion, a duet of light,
Fusing hydrogen, oh what a sight!
Helium chuckles, helium sighs,
Painting the heavens with giggles and cries!

Primal energy, a party to keep,
A pulsing heartbeat, a cosmic leap.
Join in the riot of stellar ballet,
In this interstellar, lively display!

The Sound of Universes Colliding

Booom! goes the cosmos, a thunderous cheer,
Colliding and crashing, oh what's that we hear?
Stars in a tussle, galaxies play,
With comets and asteroids joining the fray!

Splat! goes the nebula, colors so bright,
A canvas of chaos, a wild starfight.
Galaxy giggles echo, a multi-sound feast,
As matter and energy shake hands in the east!

Swirls of starstuff, dancing in space,
They tumble and twirl in this cosmic race.
Such pushing and shoving, who's winning today?
It's a merry-go-round in the Milky Way!

Finally landing, as laughter subsides,
The universe whispers, its joy never hides.
Let's toast to the chaos, so bold and so free,
For the sound of creation's pure harmony!

Tapestry of Time and Space

Threaded in stardust, a quilt of delight,
The fabric of cosmos woven so tight.
Each stitch a moment, each color, a tale,
Warp and weft dancing, as stars paint the veil!

The tickle of timelines, playful and spry,
Weaving through ages, both low and high.
A yawn from a planet, a giggle from light,
Dancing through ages, not wasting their flight!

Comets with sequins, and planets with flair,
Twirl through the galaxies, without a care.
Space-time is giggling, it knows how to jest,
In this humor-filled quilt, we're all but guests!

So grab a few threads, and join in the cheer,
We're stitching the cosmos, so far and yet near.
A tapestry glowing, with laughter embraced,
In the grandest adventure, we all are well-placed!

Celestial Whispers

In the sky, a cosmic joke,
Stars are laughing, can't revoke.
Planets twirl in silly dance,
Galaxies spin, it's all by chance.

Comets zoom with tails so bright,
Moon's got jokes that take flight.
Asteroids roll their eyes in space,
While black holes give a dark embrace.

Nebulas puff, all filled with cheer,
Winking at us, do they hear?
Gravity falls, a comedic pull,
Math and science — never dull!

So let us toast to cosmic fun,
Time and space, a wild run.
With every pulse, a universe wide,
In laughter's arms, we all abide.

Echoes of the Cosmic Dawn

Once upon a cosmic seed,
Stars were born from laughter's need.
The universe held a silly grin,
As light and matter jumped right in.

Galaxies clashed with a giggle,
Eons passed with a cosmic wiggle.
Planets formed in a playful haze,
Spinning tales of their own phase.

Time ticked on, a cheeky tease,
Creating wonders, aiming to please.
Supernovae burst, a riotous cheer,
Stardust spreading far and near.

Each echo heard throughout the void,
A joyful shout, never destroyed.
In the fabric of space, jokes intertwine,
Crafting a universe, both random and fine.

Stardust Serenade

Oh stardust, a quirky mess,
Floating by, we must confess.
With each twinkle, tales unfold,
A cosmic serenade, bright and bold.

Asteroids hum a silly tune,
Making music with the moon.
Saturn's rings, a dance of glee,
Catch a beat, come dance with me!

Cosmic rays fly, what a blast!
Creating laughter, unsurpassed.
Black holes burp, it's quite absurd,
In the universe, joy's preferred.

So let's groove to the stellar sound,
Where humor in space is always found.
With every spark, a chuckle's born,
In the night sky, we're reborn.

The Birth of Light

From darkness came a bright delight,
A spark of joy, igniting light.
Photon pranks in cosmic play,
Illuminating night and day.

A laugh erupted, the void awoke,
The universe burst, like a joke.
Stars blushed down in radiant hues,
While time danced in absurd reclues.

Lightyears traveled, with jokes untold,
Shining bright, never cold.
Waves of giggles fill the air,
With every twinkle, we all share.

So here's to light, our cosmic muse,
Crafting laughter, no one can refuse.
In this wild show, let's unite,
Celebrating the birth of light.

Radiant Ripples of Creation

In the void, a sneeze by fate,
Stars danced up, oh can't wait!
They twirled like kids on a spree,
Spinning gas, with glee and glee.

Planets popped like popcorn's cheer,
Galaxies giggled, all was clear.
A cosmic chef, with spice and fun,
Stirring chaos, under a sun!

Orchestration of the First Flame

A spark ignites, with zest and zing,
Funny firecrackers, they take wing.
Comets laugh, with tails so bright,
    Fizzling wonders in the night.

"Look at me!" one nebula shouts,
"I'm a cloud, with silly doubts!"
A stellar symphony starts to play,
Comedic cosmos, humorous sway.

Cosmic Waltz in the Void

In the darkness, a waltz began,
Galaxies gracefully took a stand.
Space-time twisted, spun with flair,
Stars atop, a whimsical pair.

"Hey there, black hole, spin me 'round!"
Said a star with a twinkly sound.
The universe giggled, swayed with pride,
In this grand dance, all could glide.

Harmonies of the Early Cosmos

Harmonies hummed in the radiant dawn,
Planets laughed as they were drawn.
"Catch me if you can, I'm on a roll!"
Echoes of joy through the cosmic stroll.

A quasar winked, like a sly friend,
"This expansion? It'll never end!"
With each note, the void sang bright,
A silly serenade, pure delight.

Symphony of the Expanding Universe

In the void, a balloon did grow,
Stars took a breath, oh how they glow!
Galaxies danced to a cosmic tune,
While meteors grooved, 'neath the silver moon.

Planets spun in a wobbly whirl,
Comets passed by with a cheeky twirl,
Gravity laughed, pulling all down,
While black holes joked, 'You'll never drown!'

Space is a party with twinkling lights,
Aliens sing on surprising nights,
Each burst of energy, a pop or a snap,
The universe laughs, "Come take a nap!"

So here we dance in this cosmic play,
With stardust jokes that never decay,
We toast to the cosmos, loud and clear,
With laughter that echoes, far and near!

Cosmic Journeys Through Time

Time travelers ride on a solar breeze,
Wearing space suits that look like cheese,
With clocks that tick to a funky beat,
They glide through planets, oh what a feat!

Paradoxical tales of yore unfold,
Where history's secrets are funny and bold,
Dinosaurs danced to a rock-n-roll vibe,
While future folks zoom by, high on a fiber tribe!

Black holes whisper, 'Hey, don't look back!'
As time loops twist in a fancy track,
Past meets the future in a playful clash,
With jokes about parking in a cosmic stash!

So pack your bags; let's hit the stars,
With laughter alive, we'll soar beyond Mars,
Through time and space, we'll sing and play,
On a journey of fun, come join the sway!

Melodies of the Night Sky

The stars croon softly in the night,
As planets hum with delight,
Nebulae flaunt their colorful glow,
In a jam session, putting on a show!

Saturn plays bass with its ring so wide,
While Jupiter drums on its stormy ride,
Uranus strums with a twisty string,
In the cosmic choir, they all sing!

Shooting stars make a wishful sound,
Tickling comets that zoom around,
The universe sways in a humorous jig,
As aliens join with a goofy gig!

So listen here under this velvet dome,
Where melodies soar and laughter roams,
The night sky revels in its cosmic art,
A playful symphony that warms the heart!

From Silence to Song

Once it was quiet, a still dark maze,
Until the universe caught fire and sways,
With a pop and a flair, sound took its stand,
Turning whispers of nothing into a band!

A symphony swirled from the chaos' wake,
As laughter erupted, the silence would break,
With planets twirling, a vibrant parade,
From void to a tune, the magic was made!

Lightyears stretched in a jazzy line,
Where light took center, oh how it would shine,
With cosmic notes that echo and play,
An aria of wonder in a bright display!

So raise a glass to this jubilant spree,
Where silence was lost to harmony's glee,
From quiet beginnings to catchy refrains,
The universe sings, and the joy remains!

Cosmic Verse

In the start, a sneeze so grand,
All the stars held hands.
Galaxies popped like popcorn,
And the universe was reborn.

Planets danced in a swirling spree,
Jupiter laughed, "Look at me!"
The sun wore shades, so cool and bright,
While comets zoomed with pure delight.

Asteroids rolled like a bowling ball,
Hoping to not hit a cosmic wall.
Black holes winked in a cheeky way,
"Come closer, it's fun!" they'd say.

The Milky Way played hide and seek,
Elusive stars, so antique.
With a twinkle, they sparkled and shone,
In this wondrous vast unknown.

Lullaby of Light

Twinkling stars sing a gentle tune,
Under the watchful, smiling moon.
Galaxies hum as they glide,
In cosmic dreams, they take a ride.

Planets giggle in a playful race,
While comets blush, leaving a trace.
Light-years pass with a giggly frown,
Wormholes wrinkle, stretching down.

Meteor showers fall like confetti,
Celestial events can get quite messy.
Asteroids joke, 'Watch out below!'
As they tumble, putting on a show.

In the cradle of space, laughter reigns,
With cosmic jokes filling the veins.
A lullaby of light, so full of cheer,
In the universe, we hold so dear.

Celestial Chorus

Shooting stars sing in harmony,
While the universe throws a jamboree.
Nebulas swirl in vibrant hues,
Creating colors no one can refuse.

Saturn spins with a ringside flair,
While Venus winks with a sultry stare.
Cosmic choirs belt out a tune,
In the heart of the galaxy, under the moon.

A comet's tail is a party hat,
While black holes shout, "What's up with that?"
The cosmos chuckles, a vast array,
Enticing laughter, night and day.

In the celestial waltz, we find our place,
Joined in the dance of time and space.
Every star a note, every planet a line,
In the chorus of galaxies, so divine.

Cradle of the Constellations

Once upon a time in cosmic play,
Stars were born from a mischievous ray.
The cradle rocked in a cheerful sway,
As Mercury teased, 'I'm not here to stay!'

Andromeda winks, 'Do you see me shine?'
While Pegasus gallops, feeling divine.
Orion flexes his stellar might,
As the cosmos giggles at his prideful sight.

With cosmic dust in a swirling twirl,
Galactic parties made the stardust whirl.
A clap of thunder, the universe cheered,
In the cradle of night, all fears disappeared.

Every twinkle a joke, every spark a grin,
In this cosmic cradle, we all fit in.
With laughter echoing through space and time,
The universe dances to its own rhyme.

Lightyear Lyrics

In the cosmos, stars like to chat,
Planets dance in a goofy hat.
Galaxies swirl with a wink and a grin,
What a party, let the fun begin!

Asteroids tumble, oh what a sight,
Comets zipped past in the moonlight.
They giggle and laugh, a cosmic show,
Even black holes join in the flow!

Saturn rings swing like a jump rope,
Neptune decided it would be dope.
To host a bash for the astrological crew,
With snacks made of stardust, just for you!

From far-off stars to the nearest one,
Space is vibrant, full of fun.
So come, float in this joyful spree,
And dance among the stars with glee!

Astral Echoes

Echoes of laughter in cosmic air,
Neat little planets without a care.
Shooting stars streak by with a joke,
In the galaxy's laughter, they all soak.

Supernovae burst with delight,
Twinkling like candles on a birthday night.
Quasars winking, oh what a scene,
An interstellar party like you've never seen!

Meteor showers shower gifts from above,
As nebulae twirl in a dance of love.
Join the intergalactic silly spree,
Where even the dark matter wants to be free!

With every star, there's a tale to tell,
Of cosmic chuckles, we know so well.
So let your spirit soar and unite,
In the soulful echoes of the starry night!

From Dust to Harmony

From cosmic dust we are spun,
In this universe of whimsy and fun.
Stars burst forth, glittering bright,
Each one says, 'Hey, let's unite!'

Galactic giggles travel afar,
With spinning planets and a wishing star.
Like children at play, they twist and twirl,
In this cosmic dance, let laughter unfurl!

Gravity pulls but can't keep us down,
As rockets zoom, we laugh and frown.
With space dust sprinkled all about,
We find our joy without a doubt!

In the great void where wonders unfold,
Stories of chaos and humor told.
Embrace the journey; no need to worry,
For laughter's the heart of our cosmic story!

The Symphony of Space

In the orchestra of the night,
Planets play with all their might.
Saxophones made of comets' tails,
While stardust hums in cosmic trails.

The sun's a drummer, booming loud,
While moons sway gently, veiled in a shroud.
Asteroids pluck the strings of fate,
And meteors crash in a grand soirée!

With harmony rising, meteors prance,
In the symphony of space, they dance.
Each note a twinkle, a wink, a cheer,
Resonating joy from far and near!

So join the concert, let your heart race,
In the beautiful madness of this vast place.
The universe sings, a melody bright,
Forever play on in the starry night!

Notes on the Event Horizon

In the cosmic dance, things twist and twirl,
No time for worries, just give it a whirl!
Stars steal the show with a comical flare,
Even black holes laugh, if you catch them aware.

Gravity's a joker, pulling us tight,
Tugs on your socks, what a silly sight!
Planets in orbit, a merry-go-round,
Spinning in circles, where laughs can be found.

Asteroids shout out, 'Hey, I'm still here!'
While comets zip by with a giggle and cheer.
The universe winks, with a wink so divine,
Saying, "Hold my drink, it's party time!"

In this zany expanse, every quasar beams,
Cosmic jokes echo in starlit dreams.
So raise up your glass to the night and the light,
Laughter's the spark that ignites the night!

Dreamscapes of the Expanding Realm

In realms of dreams, the stars play darts,
Bouncing off planets, they've all got their parts.
Galaxies gather for a game of charades,
Laughing in clusters, avoiding cascades.

A nebula giggles, all cloud-like and shy,
While moons play hopscotch in the deep velvet sky.
Comets' sleek tails draw smiley faces,
Swirling around, making cosmic embraces.

Pulsars pulse rhythm with beats so absurd,
Echoing punchlines that haven't been heard.
The universe grins, with a sparkle and twist,
Reminding us all that no one's dismissed.

So wake from your slumber, you stargazing chap,
Join in the laughter, embrace the mishap!
With imagination sprawling, the fun never ends,
In the vast cosmic tapestry, all are our friends.

Celestial Echoes: A Universe Awakes

Morning has come to the vast cosmic bay,
Where stars brush their teeth, and meteors play.
Galaxies yawn, stretching wide from their dreams,
As cosmic comedians devise wild schemes.

Asteroids talk in their raspy old tones,
Swapping goofy stories, like old pals on phones.
The sun hugs the planets, it's warm and so bright,
"Shine on, my children, it's time for the light!"

Rocket ships zoom with a zany flair,
Dodging the laughter that fills up the air.
Cosmic dust sprinkles like glitter on fun,
Mischief at play, till the day is all done.

In the whirl of existence, with whimsy and cheer,
Every quark is chuckling, so pull up a chair.
Join in the rapture, embrace the expanse,
In the echoes of cosmos, everyone can dance!

Radiance from a Fading Past

Once in a flash, the universe bright,
Sparks from the chaos ignited the night.
Waves of the past chuckle softly and low,
As echoes remind us of how things must go.

Photons in jammies skip past with a grin,
Cuddling with darkness, where does it begin?
Time tickles our senses, a playful old friend,
Riding on laughter as we all twist and bend.

Gravity whispers, with warmth in its tone,
Saying, "Hey buddy, you're never alone!"
Whirling through time, in a cosmic parade,
Triggers for giggles, not just being played.

So let us connect with the light and the past,
Embrace every moment, make each moment last.
In this dazzling space where our stories collide,
Laughter's a language, our hearts open wide!

The Poetry of Pulsars

In the cosmos, twinkling lights,
Pulsars dance on starry nights.
Their rhythms bounce, a cosmic joke,
Winking at us through the smoke.

Galaxies swirl, a dizzy spin,
Stars giggle, they're made of win.
A cosmic play, each flash a quirk,
As spacetime bends, we all go berserk.

Planets wobble, take a bow,
Orbiting suns with a silly wow.
Asteroids laugh as they pass by,
Chasing comets that whiz on high.

So let's toast with cosmic cheer,
To the laughter of the universe near.
For in this grand and funny scene,
Eternal joy reigns supreme!

Symphonies of Stardom

Stars up high, they sing their tune,
A symphony beneath the moon.
With twinkling notes and cosmic flair,
The Milky Way hums, without a care.

Nebulas swirl in vibrant hue,
While black holes play peek-a-boo.
Shooting stars take center stage,
Performing pranks as they engage.

Celestial hands clap in delight,
As quasars beam with all their might.
Gravity's bass thumps with a grin,
While the universe spins, it's bound to win!

So let's dance to the cosmic beat,
With starry rhythms—oh, so sweet!
The symphonies of space unfold,
Where every quasar's a story told.

Celestial Soundscapes

In the void, a chorus sounds,
Galactic giggles all around.
With comets soaring, laughter flows,
Astral antics, as everyone knows!

Wormholes whirl with a comic twist,
As planets spin, they can't resist.
Their orbits wobble, such funny sights,
Riding space waves like kite-flying flights.

Solar flares flicker and tease,
While cosmic clouds drift with ease.
Echoes of laughter fill the air,
In this vast playground, void of care.

So join the fun, in starlit dives,
As we celebrate these cosmic lives.
With humor bright in the night sky,
The universe plays, oh my, oh my!

Timeless Waltz

In the dark, what a fuss,
Stars giggle, just for us.
Galaxies spin with delight,
Dancing in the endless night.

Atoms cheer, they jump and play,
Quarks and leptons in ballet.
With a twirl and a spin, so bright,
They twinkle in their cosmic flight.

Planets laugh, they know their role,
Round and round, they rock and roll.
In this dance of space and time,
Every movement feels sublime.

Chaos reigns, what a blast,
Nothing's simple, nothing's fast.
Yet amid the swirling mess,
We find joy, we must confess.

The Universe's Narrative

Once upon a time, they say,
A burst of light led the way.
From atoms scattered far and wide,
In each nook, a spark of pride.

Stars exchanged their silly jokes,
While comets played tag with the folks.
They spun tales of ancient lore,
In this cosmic, noisy store.

Black holes had their secrets, deep,
While Martians danced, no time for sleep.
Galaxies took a grand old bow,
As the universe laughed out loud.

Time ticked on, what a scene,
Where space's oddities convene.
In this grand and wacky play,
We're just props in a cosmic sway.

Melodies of Matter

With a bang, the fun begins,
A note from chaos, tune that wins.
Cosmic strings strum a happy song,
Resonating all night long.

Dark matter hums a silly tune,
While neutrinos dance under the moon.
Electrons twirl, they spin about,
Creating smiles without a doubt.

Every atom claps in glee,
As the cosmos sings, oh, so free.
Giggles echo from star to star,
Universe's soundtrack, near and far.

Jumping particles spin with pride,
Waltzing on this cosmic ride.
Amidst the sounds of playful cheer,
We laugh together, no fear here.

Sounds of the Ether

In the void, can you hear?
Laughter echoes, never sheer.
Whispers of quarks, a silly show,
Giggles ripple through the flow.

Shooting stars make wishes bright,
As they dance across the night.
Supernovae pop and fizz,
Creating chuckles just like this.

Cosmic rays are tickling eyes,
As nebulae fluff up the skies.
Every atom's in a jest,
In this wild, eternal fest.

So join the fun, don't lag behind,
In this universe, feel aligned.
From the tiniest, smallest start,
Comes the joy, a cosmic art.

Tones of the Eternal Cosmos

In the dark we all collide,
Galaxies take a wild ride,
Asteroids dance with comets' tails,
While aliens swap their funny tales.

Planets wobble in confused glee,
Orbiting drinks of cosmic tea,
Black holes burp with a thundering sound,
A cosmic party goes round and round.

Neutron stars wear their best hats,
While meteors play like silly cats,
Lunar bunnies jump through the night,
Comparing who can shine the brightest light.

Gravity pulls on moonlit dreams,
As cosmic laughter always beams,
In this universe of endless play,
We sing and giggle the night away.

Cosmic Whispers

Among the stars, a secret scheme,
Whispers float like a silly dream,
Pluto jokes with Jupiter's flair,
While Venus brings a silly chair.

Meteor showers rain down pranks,
Creating chaos in the flanks,
Aliens chuckle, passing by,
With rubber ducks that float on high.

The Milky Way spins with delight,
As suns debate who shines more bright,
Constellations play hide and seek,
Creating shapes that make us weep.

Galactic giggles echo wide,
In this vast and fun-filled ride,
So grab a star and join the game,
The cosmos is a funny frame.

Celestial Crescendo

Stars court the comets in a waltz,
While musical moons strike cosmic faults,
A symphony of bizarre delight,
As quarks spin jokes throughout the night.

Planets hum in silly tunes,
Dancing to the light of moons,
Astrophysicists lose their way,
As space itself begins to sway.

Sing, oh sun, of cosmic cheer,
And let the dark matter draw near,
For black holes sing, though they eat fast,
It's a meal that's bound to last.

Watch the universe in its quirk,
Voices rise from the dark, a perk,
In this grand celestial show,
We giggle as we swirl and glow.

Stardust Melodies

In stardust fields, we trip along,
Singing silly cosmic songs,
Imaginary friends parade,
While shooting stars begin to fade.

Nebulae cheer with a burst of joy,
As comets tease the black hole's ploy,
With twinkling eyes, they jig and prance,
Creating waves of a cosmic dance.

Planets mingle, sharing jokes,
While distant quasars light the folks,
Galaxies giggle, swirling bright,
Under the blanket of endless night.

So let the melodies soar and dive,
In this universe where we thrive,
With laughter woven through every star,
Stardust dreams shall take us far.

The Song of Stars

In the dark where starlights twinkle,
A dance of gas clouds, oh so sprightly.
Planets waltz in elliptical paths,
While comets tickle with their fiery laughs.

Galaxies sway with a cosmic cheer,
Shooting stars giggle, drawing near.
A quasar's joke, oh, it's out of sight,
Making black holes blush in the night.

Asteroids crammed with candy dreams,
Flavors of cosmos, bursting at the seams.
They share their treats with every child,
Riding moonbeams, all wild and mild.

So laugh with the universe, join the spree,
Where laughter echoes, endlessly free.
A cosmic chorus, forever we'll sing,
Through the vastness, let joy take wing.

Dreams in the Dark

Beneath the blankets of shimmering night,
Whispers of stardust fill the flight.
Alien critters with googly eyes,
Tell silly tales of pizza in the skies.

Nebulae giggle at a clumsy star,
Who trips on a light beam, it's bizarre!
Time ticks funny in this cosmic nook,
While cosmic kittens play with a starry book.

Planets plot their next big scheme,
To throw a party, oh what a dream!
With asteroids dancing, oh so spry,
And meteors wearing ties, oh my!

So drift into dreams, let the laughter flow,
In the universe's embrace, let joy grow.
For every moment, a giggle might spark,
In the deep and cozy, warm and dark.

Waves of Existence

Surfing through space on quantum waves,
Jellyfish particles, how each one behaves!
Gravity giggles, pulls with a grin,
While galaxies spin, let the fun begin!

Ripples of matter, what a funny sight,
The universe chuckles in pure delight.
Photon prances, dances with light,
Creating a rave that lasts all night.

Each atom grins at the chaos it made,
In this cosmic carnival, no need to fade.
Quarks in a conga line, feel the beat,
While spacetime churns in a quirky feat!

So ride the waves with a giggly cheer,
For existence is funny when you're near.
The universe dances, in colorful play,
In the frolic of stars, come what may!

Cosmic Resonance

Tune into the cosmos, hear the sound,
While quarks jingle, joy does abound.
Strings vibrating with a happy tone,
Laughter echoes from the great unknown.

Planets hum a merry little tune,
Their orbits spinning beneath the moon.
Black holes chuckle, sucking in jest,
As galaxies wink, never a rest.

With every pulsar's playful beat,
A symphony of chaos, oh so sweet!
Singing stars twirl in cosmic delight,
As the universe dances with sheer excitement.

So find your rhythm in the cosmic dance,
Embrace every chuckle, give it a chance.
For in the resonance of life's grand song,
A funny universe, where we all belong.

The Luminous Overture

In a universe so wide, they dance and sway,
Galaxies twirl, in a cosmic ballet.
Stars throw confetti, in a radiant spree,
While black holes giggle at their lack of a key.

Planets play hide and seek, round and round,
Asteroids join in with a thumping sound.
Comets chase dreams, in a glittering rush,
Making light of time, in a stellar hush.

Nebulas lounge, in colors so bright,
Whispering secrets of the endless night.
While quasars joke, like cosmic clowns,
Spreading laughter through the celestial towns.

So raise a glass to the silliness vast,
In a universe where the fun's unsurpassed.
Here's to the wonders, the quirks, the flair,
In this wild life where we all have a share.

Notes from the Celestial Abyss

From deep space comes a giggle, echoing low,
A serenade sung by the stars in a row.
The moon winks slyly, with a wink and a grin,
Saying, "Why don't you join? Let the fun begin!"

Black holes ponder, 'What's on today's menu?'
Entropical snacks, with a side of sun dew.
While nebulae swirl with hues of delight,
Chasing away darkness, embracing the light.

Bits of stardust with a chuckle and glee,
Share stories of chaos, of snacks lost at sea.
Astronauts giggle with gravity's tricks,
As they float through the void, in their funny little kicks.

Each comet's a joke, whizzing by with a flare,
A smile in the cosmos, floating everywhere.
So tune in your heart to this whimsical creed,
For laughter and joy are the universe's needs.

A Dance of Stars and Shadows

Step right up to the cosmic show,
Where stars cha-cha and shadows toe-to-toe.
The night sky's a stage, so come take a glance,
As meteors wobble in their clumsy dance.

Jupiter bumps into his friend Saturn,
While Venus giggles from behind a lantern.
The galaxies chuckle as they spin and sway,
In this stellar soirée, come join the play!

Twinkling lights burst with laughter and cheer,
Echoing secrets only we can hear.
Each twinkling star, a judge at the ball,
With heavenly giggles, they invite us all.

So leap into darkness, don't be slow,
In this cosmic carnival, let your heart glow.
Stars and shadows are here to amaze,
As they jive through the night in glittering displays.

Birth of Infinity

In a swirl of giggles, the cosmos was spun,
A birth full of mischief, oh what a fun run!
With quarks and photons prancing about,
Even the void couldn't help but shout.

The universe grinned with a cheeky delight,
As electrons played tag in the fabric of night.
Time jumped around like it was on a spree,
Making memories blossom—oh, can't you see?

Constellations wink with a starlit jest,
As galaxies burst, all tangled and pressed.
Every flicker is a secret, a wink, a tease,
In a jubilant dance where time bends with ease.

So as this grand tale of chaos unfurls,
In the giggle of space, let laughter twirls.
We celebrate life as a cosmic potluck,
Filled with humor and joy, where we're all in luck.

www.ingramcontent.com/pod-product-compliance
Lightning Source LLC
Chambersburg PA
CBHW071854160426
43209CB00003B/557